Garden Earth

ALLANA RAINE KING

Copyright ©Allana Raine King 2022

ISBN: 9798442960693

Allana Raine King (4th June 1999 – 12th October 2018)

Allana grew up in the City of Bristol, England, UK.

She achieved excellent exam grades at Bristol Free School and carried on to the sixth form at St Brendan's College, where she obtained the grades to further her career at Kingston upon Thames University to study Creative Writing and English Literature.

Allana loved writing, whether it be poems, songs, stories or her life experiences. Every spare moment she was writing - it was her 'happy place'. One of her poems was published in the Teen Poets 'Youthful Expressions' at the tender age of 14 - called 'Consciousness'. Between studying she would attend open mic poetry sessions and perform on stage, which came naturally to her. Her skills obtained through ballet at 3 years of age and performing in school plays helped to give her the confidence to express herself.

It was her destiny and purpose in life to be a writer and she hoped her poems and stories would give joy and inspiration to everyone who read them. Her outlook on life was to live it well and always care for others less fortunate than herself. Allana felt blessed and thankful for her life. She was beautiful not only on the outside but within; she was in touch with her spirituality and of others. She loved the company of children and animals and had a special connection with them. She was passionate about cooking, and being vegetarian, loved to create nutritious dishes, particularly vegetable curries.

In 2018, the year she was looking forward to starting University, Allana became ill with Encephalitis, an autoimmune disease where the body's immune system attacks healthy cells and tissues in the brain or spinal cord. It was sudden, brutal and totally unexpected and changed our lives forever. Allana said she never felt alone in her struggle with her illness and was blessed to have the love and support of her family and friends at this time.

Allana was true to her values and beliefs and was her own person and grew to be a strong independent woman. She was brave, happy and intelligent and although her life was short, she lived a fulfilled one. As her family, we are very grateful, honoured and blessed to have been a part of her life. Each one of us will carry forward our special memories of her forever. Allana is an inspiration to us all to live our lives to the full.

I dedicate this book
With love in my heart
To my family and all my readers

Thank you to:

The Encephalitis Society

Marion Ashton and Christopher Sanderson, truly grateful

Allana, for her inspiration and brilliant work

This is a remarkable collection from a gifted young poet. The final poem 'A Story to Tell' portrays her strength, dignity and imaginative skill – 'A light that sparkles off a navy sea. A person to be remembered and told.'

Marion Ashton

Contents:

SWEET TOOTH	17
ENGLAND	18
WHAT A WOMAN	19
THE DREAM MAN	20
I'M LOVING IT	21
YOUNG	22
PARIS	23
AWAKENING	24
JANUARY	25
BOY	26
OUTSIDE	27
MAYBE	28
MR O'MALLEY	29
MR TRUMPET MAN	30
SALTY BLUES	31
HANDS	32
GARDEN EARTH	33
NIGHT	34
THYSELF	35
STILLNESS	36
THE FALL	37
REMEMBER WHAT YOU CAME FOR	38
STAR CHILD	39
VEGETARIAN	40
MILK MORNING	41
BLUE BUBBLE	42
A GREEN LIGHT	43
11:11	44
THOUGHTS	45
HIM	46
A SILVER LIGHT	47
MARCH	48
NUMEROLOGY	49
JE REVE (I dream)	50
A FEW WORDS	51
I AM SORRY LIFE DID NOT GO AS PLANNED	52
TELL ME	53
SOMEWHERE NEW	54
MIRRORED SELF	55

REPLAY THE SONG	56
SUNRISE	57
THIS MOMENT	58
THE PRICE TO PAY	59
UNSPOKEN	60
SLIPPERY NET	61
I WISH I WAS THERE	62
STREET NAMES	64
THE WORLD STAGE	65
WORDS	66
THE TRIUMPHAL ARCH	67
NOISELESS BATTLE	68
CARTE BLANCHE	69
YOUNG DESIRE	70
POLITICAL PUPPETS	71
FLY FURTHER AND FAR	72
NEW LIGHT CALLS	73
LUNA	74
MATERIAL MAYHEM	75
RECYCLED PATTERN	76
DOES LOVE CONQUER ALL	77
THE WEIGHT OF DARKER DAYS	78
APRIL	79
A SERIES OF COINCIDENCES	80
END OF EXAMS	81
NEW WORLDS	82
UNTITLED	83
CURRENTS OF CHANGE	87
ILLUSION	88
FALLING DOMINOES	89
WE ARE ALL TREASURED	90
A STORY TO TELL	91

SWEET TOOTH

The substitute of happiness
A guilty pleasure she seeks to devour
In less than an hour
She'll feel no joy
She must contain her sin
Before it devours her
The substitute of happiness
It is non-renewable
For this happiness is only an illusion
As she intakes the chocolate confusion
She believes she is in heaven
And as the bars unfold
The gates close
The substitute of happiness
Years go by and she swims in a sea of wrappers
And they flapper as she splashes past
She knows she won't last
She can't breathe anymore
Drowning in a swallow addiction
Whilst everyone else can float
But she's praying for a boat to save her
The chocolate chomps on
And once a girl
So full of dreams
Was enslaved in chocolate chains

ENGLAND

The concrete jungle
A sophisticated chaos
Structured upon mother's nature
Like old Babylon
The prosperity helps the rich
And defines the poor, old and weak
Would it be so bleak?
To say its entirety is
The blood and bones of so many
Who gained no less pride
Of an animal worked to death
From hard labour from dawn till night
With its high buildings
It appears fair and majestic
It hides its truth and history
Even from its own
But carefully I watch alone
And discover the true meaning
The concrete jungle

WHAT A WOMAN

She puts on a smile
And the world is fooled
Her grace sweeps her
She glides across the earth
Her words are meaningless
But her eyes make you learn
That she is beautiful
Utterly breathless
And you forget she's merely a being
She is a goddess
An alien
He'll never understand her
Why she seems so far away
She kisses him goodbye
He tells her she's the one
But she's only with him
For a bit of fun

THE DREAM MAN

He was given a job
A duty
He was a soldier
Prepared to go in for a fight
He never asked for it
It was difficult
Being the man of the night
Carefully dropping dreams
Like teardrops
So delicate and pure
It was beautiful
And terrifying
He felt the allure
He couldn't go wrong
He was a soldier
But what if he did
Nightmares would fall
Quickly
Perhaps onto a little kid
He was given a job
A duty
Even an honourable kilt
But all the dream man felt
Was lots of guilt

I'M LOVING IT

He tells her what he wants
She then shuts up
She does as he says and pulls a smile
She's polite
And he's desperate
Two worlds collide for a while
She gives him what he wants
And he gives it back
He wants something else
Maybe some fries with that
She tells him how much
He didn't think it was free
The love for Macdonald's
Ends so happily

YOUNG

I gave you my heart
Thinking this was for the start
Of something new
But you withdrew
Something more
You opened the door
And stole part of me
Then buzzed off like a bee
I was upset
Filling my heart up as if in debt
I didn't know
That people come and they go
That love is blind
And you'll only find
True happiness through despair
And love is the only repair
Like chemical magic dust
You'll only ever see the lust
But true love is the empty bottle
That we wish to throttle

PARIS

Golden chains
Locked as love stains
Across bridges that will remain
Until eternity is claimed
As lovers lock their love
Like a promise for the above
And as the Tower watches
On all fours
We close the doors of reality
For heartbreakers never occur
And cheaters are just an old rumour
And the broken perceptions
Is what beauty is left
The fantasy
The dream
Now this is why the Tower beams

AWAKENING

If reality is a perception
Then it is only a possibility
Out of infinities
As he sees'
What his conscience believes
His mind is at ease
For it is easy
To except the reality, one has created
He is limited
Concept constipated
In an igloo ignorance
He is more than he knows
His conscious glows
His heart feels
Yet his mind doesn't know what is real

JANUARY

Fluffy flakes
Of heavens carpet fell from the sky
In a blur of white
The sky grew tight clouds
Which blanketed the sky
From the unmistakable cold
Of January
From a crying despair of snow
The clouds broke apart
Recalling the heart of the sky
Then everything was blue
And new again
Like the unmistakable start
Of January

BOY

You will never understand
Or you will
To give back from what you steal
What is the price of a heart?
Pain stronger than 1000 stabbing darts
It was one moment
One now
Told me to kiss you to show you how
I laughed and you smiled
Desire grew wild
You leaned in and I stayed
You betrayed
I played
You took it
But before I could see
You had the lock and key
With my heart in your hands
You still didn't understand
That's what makes me cry
No matter how hard you try
It kills me inside
You should have taken your time
What is the price of a heart?
If you steal, don't start

OUTSIDE

The sun blinded me
For it wasn't sunny at all
And as far as my deception
Outside was colder than death
But warmer than death's breath
For flowers bloomed
And the world was tuned in joy
People played with toys
That floated in the sky
Which were cold lies
For outside was colder than death
But warmer than death's breath
Next time
I'll take a jacket

MAYBE

Maybe I love you
Behind perplex pulses
And false hopes
That drip wet with lies
Tightened in bow ties
Completing his suit
Your suit
It is I
Doubtfully correct
From the day we met
My heart danced within a percussion
That strayed my mind into a discussion
Do I love you
Do I not
And the questions do not stop
Denial, oh look what I have become
Lost within the momentum of your soul
I fear I shall never grow old
Of this feeling
Dreaming
Maybe I love you

MR O'MALLEY

The cats licked their lips
As the saxophone swung its hits
The sugary brush of drums
The cats bit their thumbs
As the trumpet hushed
The mice began to rush
Let's make a run
A serious case of jazz fun
Each note fell onto another
The cat said hello little brother
Holding onto the mouse's tail
Jazz will never fail
With a cheeky blue
The cat sees you
Nodding your head
Now the mouse is dead

MR TRUMPET MAN

His silver hair and pointy nose
Back and forth before he rose
Centre stage
Told the sax to behave
Mr Trumpet man
Teach me if you can
Sexy flavour, you make me stare
With all your jazz flare
Mr Trumpet man
Why are you so modest?
With a sound so pure and honest
I love your soul
You fill my cup whole
Mr Trumpet man
Play it for me
Say it for me
In all your words of jazz

SALTY BLUES

Echoing through the city night
With a bass so still
You make the cold chill
Salty blues
Tell me did you lose your love?
The mellow pain
In your disdain
I feel you
Salty blues
In spite of the moonlit sight
You drag your light
To a sweeter darkness
Salty blues
There is something about you
In a mysterious depth
Soak me in your wet,
Set tears
Salty blues

HANDS

Touch the tips that dip cold
On my hands
I make from these
So, hold on, squeeze, knead
The flesh against bone
Kiss the outside
Study the lines within, small, tiny and large
I cook from these
I wash from these
I wait with these hands
Little by little
So fragile and tender
The soft skin peels away
Reborn
Pulsing in the wake
Breathing on their own
These are my hands
They are mine alone

GARDEN EARTH

I have love on the carpet Earth;
Underneath the growing decay
The grey smog and foul array.
What was once;
Ripe fruits, sweet grass and blossom bloom
How much as less a grey world?
Underneath a moon
By beauty, by building and by city
Exceedingly torn and less pretty
A technological woe,
Burdened at a narrow expense
A new world
Beauty reckoned of a virtual fence
Let us watch it grow, better yet,
Let us wonder
Like curious Eve, may a woman ponder
This thick cloud, dried rivers and floods
This cost and damage paid in blood
I will not, I must not damage this garden
Utterly in truth, all that is I shall borrow
May I return without sharp sorrow
I have compassion on the carpet Earth;
Not in pity, nor duty and in a blunted heart
Though' with honour and discernment
By choice and affirmation
Not by any declamation of God;
Served only to the core of thy self-will.
I have love on the carpet Earth
Let us drink its waters
Breathe, from the garden
To restore our negligence
To an Eden, forgiven.

NIGHT

Sprinkled stars
Scatter upon the night cake
And a cherry moon on top
Sickly sweet he roams the night
Venturing the sweetie land of darkness
He sees the popping candy men
Who were calm and chocolate still
And the strawberry lace girls
Who dress to be seen
He sees the sugar energy of the night
The never-ending yellow lights
That buzz from street to street
And as the night fizzes on
The taste becomes too much
He has seen enough
But instead, he wakes up from a dream

THYSELF

They don't realise
They don't understand
Underneath this skin
I am within;
Different
Darker
When I look, God made me smarter
Than to participate the hate
Change to relate
Compensate myself
Because I know something they don't
Something they can't take
No matter how isolate and remove
Disapprove against my skin
We have all crossed blood sin
Underneath the sun eye
I am no better
I am black
The unseen, the night
Between third sight
I am black
The spiritual master, moon leader
The highest knight
I am black
Unchanged, all-seeing healer
And my power is beyond
And my power is growing
Towards an untold truth
I am black
Expansion throughout the universe

STILLNESS

It was real, stillness, the presence of affinity
In the freshness I was alive
Beckoning my being
The world was no longer what it had once been
Sat alone
Transparent and simple
Each moment as it comes
I watched, I felt, I am
Whisper to me
In the stillness of the present
It is not something you can teach
Entire peace

THE FALL

Take the first step my dear
Don't let me fall
Weightless
Underneath you
Take your image
Take your body
Now push away
We can't stay here forever
Broken wings
Beaten
In banished hours
Without power
Blinded
Through the fall

REMEMBER WHAT YOU CAME FOR

I undressed your skin
Slim skeleton
Pressed against fear
A cold heart
Covered in muscle
Dig deeper beyond bone
A king of thrones
Not a lover
We made movement
In these white covers
A sticky romance
Glued to our hearts
Keep marching the pain
So, may, that I can feel
What left remains

STAR CHILD

Light in the flesh suit
An energy tower learning
Through foundations of mind
Take the time to grow truths
Seeding imaginations
Creating the life, you will
Although –
Time is not real
It is what you feel
The only importance at hand
Your intuition demands
Listen well
In order to break the spell
Stay awake, do not sleep as sheep
Dream, only to the beat of your heart
To march above the charade
Pure seeds will pave
The highest path

VEGETARIAN

Why I don't eat meat?
The same way I do not sleep with the dead
A carcass in my body
Is the same as my bed
It is not a weight I wish to carry
Nor to share
Animals have will
Not at my expense to tear at
In ignorance with my knife and fork
To slaughter life without shame or thought
It is to understand;
Man is not owed anything
Can you eat what you cannot kill?
Each life has a purpose to fulfil
Not at the hand of man
In the vein of because we can
I do not eat meat
Goat, horse, cow, pig, lamb or sheep

MILK MORNING

The crisp of Monday
And the perpetuate drive that motors the week
I was not there in its freshness
I was alone again
Wondering why I was not on a beach
Fed up of the game, forever the same notion
It was quite frankly Monday
Bright and clear
I was certain I was not supposed to be here
In city day break
Behind the café window
Another veil between me and the world

BLUE BUBBLE

Silk freedom, never caught through skies
For all time was mine
Shape master of the day
Clouds bent to gay hearts
Melodies of nature turn inward
At the start of something new
Rightfully in tune
The birds sing and sang
A new day, a new life

A GREEN LIGHT

The past lingers like a shadow
Each corner of memories
Paint through my vision
Let go, she said
Never
And so, pictures pile
All the while haunting me
Blending through the streets
The people we meet
Ghosts of whom you have met
Not here, but there
Perhaps in a green light
Ever green
Flickering between illusion
Memories or lies
I battle to believe
A past you conquer to achieve
All green and murky

11:11

I see you brightly
You are a painting
Amazing and true
Perhaps you are new
Colours to my eyes
Flesh coated disguise
A woman of two
Inside and outside
A light and darkness
A void in her heart
Skipping through madness
Smile before they see
Criss cross never leave
Tip toe and achieve
All from inside you
But it is all fear
Time will tell you now
How much I love you
With more understanding
It is clear you are here
Fulfilling your purpose
Like a goddess from space
Your soul is to my taste
Human beauty and shape
Dimensions and echoes
Replace the old version
And you became a balance
And you did not know it
Testing your old beliefs
Remember that you can
Fail and try again
You are truly magic
So do not fear at all
If you do believe this
You will pass and succeed
Your heart will never bleed

THOUGHTS

Always on your mind
I'm always on your mind
Ticking against time
Don't stop because
Tomorrow is near
Run through your mind
Trip from time to time
Flip the switch
To find the light
I can't see you
When you're thinking
I can't feel you

HIM

You are brief in the movement of my years
I blink and you return
To the mind's eye you are not clear
Images blurred
Burnt love and broken sex
The flames of irony back to when we met
Itching you attention cold
Through a healing heart
You're are not the same and I know
I only show myself alone
Too many wounds to count
Through my body you entered
A love without knocking
Virginity's request
A spoiled demand for the unknown
In the sharpest hour
It was over
I felt no better or less
I got dressed, we left
That was all
A connection I hoped for
I was the fool
Too fast to feel a love
I bent down, you above
What did I expect throughout the years?
I blink and the vision is gone
You return to a stranger
So, we move on patient and afraid
Pushing through the parade of ideals
Praying the next time, we might feel
A love that we deserve

A SILVER LIGHT

A silver light in my chest
A shimmer through the grey,
You stole my lonely days
I used to dress up for no one
Searching for something
An old magic
All alone, playing with my nerve
I read for something
Café shops my third home
I don't want you to go there
But you might
It was a dark world
But I found light
So, forgive me
I don't have the answers
I'm vulnerable
Quite
Irrational sometimes
So, if I run away
Tell me you need me to stay, tell me you –

MARCH

Outside, a white form had
Absorbed the sky, as each
Flake chased the other
Tenderly, its gentle dust
Settled through the husk
Of the wind as it exhaled
In a blank blur, time
Became a colour, of one form
White land and icy streets
A flow of flake feet
Pacing the paths
There were screams
And warm laughter
Beeping horns, troubles after
The second beat of March
Nature's song of snow
Landed before us breathless
In a gentle glow

NUMEROLOGY

Naked numbers saved me
Took me in their pattern
Sequence and strings
Silver spoken
But through digital dial
Each glance and look
Checking clock
Answering my call
They have their own talk
Numbers in breath
Symbols dancing through mystic
Flashing at me as I walk
Numbers of wisdom
Numbers of spirit
A guidance of the soul
Help me make decisions
Help me to achieve my goal

JE REVE (I DREAM)

Sometimes the world bares a coldness
Rattles in my chest
Screaming how will I adapt here
I become infected with fear
Born in body, but never enough
Clothes on my back and still struggles are tough
Am I in sync to city rhythm?
Or do I drown in city tide?
Here, are we alive or do we always grind?
Softer sounds call me, unto a sweeter life
I work until the day I reach paradise

A FEW WORDS

He said, life has always been
Cyclical nature: crafting and unfolding
In kind and always seen
Dancing as fold
It is not personal
In fact, quite detached from you
It is purposeful and merciful
A vivid dream comes true
We are all but avatars
Characters that drive an unknown plot
A cast of gold stars
Filmed from a wide world shot
You give it meaning and it is worthy
Be at grace on your journey

I AM SORRY LIFE DID NOT GO AS PLANNED

You are the best you will get
Let all your colours set
Don't forget that you are beautiful
Fruitful in tools and talents truthful
Don't cry the paint in your eyes
Fly through the highest sky
Then fall in love
With all the wonders of you
You blossom in the dew of the morning
As the yolk of the sun
Showers over the rest of your body
Your journey has only begun
Now grow

TELL ME

How many versions of self have you discovered?
How many times did you die anew?
How many truths of the past have you recovered?
How many situations in which you grew?
How many times were you curious?
How many times did you fail?
How many years were you furious?
How many lives of yours lived to tell the tale?
What was most important in all?
Did you climb higher or did you fall?
Tell me, did you live off the wall?
Tell me, did you live?

SOMEWHERE NEW

You deserve all these wonderful things
And life has its ways
Distractions and delays
I want to sleep forever
With you by my side
If my mind has better places
Without familiar faces
Cotton chats, ridden rats' races –
Then I have two minds' eyes
I have two faces
Each acting in my ear
Tell me what I want to hear
That I will wake up
Somewhere new and somewhere safe
The world we made
The forbidden place
Nobody but us
But first I must trust
That all these wonderful things are here

MIRRORED SELF

So, you live in an illusion
Of colours, pictures and sounds array
Do you command your dreams?
Or are you forced to play
Why cry at the hand of shadows
Ghosts of the past shall fade away
Perhaps you are alone here
To banish fear is to reject ideas
A perfect baseless inception
Inside an immaculate concept
A mirrored self to explore
So, did you draw the fusion
Caught between reality and illusion?

REPLAY THE SONG

The sweet song of your heart
Orchestrated in visions
Plays the music of your life
You walk in melodies
You talk on the beat
The rhythm begins in your feet
Then out through your eyes
Your song cries out
In a world of noise
Aching and shaking
You keep re-playing
The sweet song of your heart
And I can hear you
And I promise to listen
To each rhythm that shakes your soul

SUNRISE

Watch the sunrise
In violet dreams
Soaked in the haze of love
We are clusters of fire light
Burning blue ablaze
From up above, in heaven's eye
Holding onto the pillars
In case we fall into a deeper space
We chase the tails
And hope to escape
Envision stretching the bond
Further and further, we find
The universe to belonging
In the hearts eye, destined divine.

THIS MOMENT

We have only now
So, I absorb all I can
Catching my breath gently
I hope to keep this forever
A space to return
When the twinkle fades into dust
And the sweet sounds turn to husk
I hope to stay here forever
In all eternity a perfect colour
This picture moment
That never ages from time to space
Caressed in my chest now
Locked living and always alive
Feeding the magic turns the tide of present
I am with you now and forever

THE PRICE TO PAY

Penniless, broke I spend more than I make
It must be shaken to me that it is not wise
Poverty is the price
Roll the dice of each action
Perhaps I do not do enough
The energy exchange, balance arrangements
Have called my bluff
Must I, pay myself first and learn wealth
To attract a higher abundance and liberty
You in all these hours of work
Money had earned me only fabric
Materials and like magic
It had left before it came
Again, it could obtain anything worth importance
In shame, cementing only dependence

UNSPOKEN

There is no grass to bear our fruit
How can we evolve now, can we plough?
When the sun balances on our heads?
We rest in ghettos and unpaid debt
Soaked in the fury of our regrets
The sky reflects the pollution of mind
The water reflects the impurities of soul
Have we not been told these truths?
So, why do we fall harder than we fly?
Elevation of time does not cease our lessons
Let us not forget;
The depth of these burdens in order grow progression
Yet all is well as all shall be
To remain patient, faithful and grateful
Free in the hands of peace
Wiser to look beyond these scenes
Than to suffer in states
To liberate all pain
To equate compassion in all
We will fall before we fly
But never to die alone

SLIPPERY NET

Whether the weather is changing
The signs had spoken
We were told but we had broken
All the importance
Crossing the boundaries of open
The unknown, slippery net of boundless
Was a beauty behind a curtain
Now but a snake in a garden
I hold steady, bracing the bend
If we are to strive, we must depend
On secure centre of self
Nothing less or nothing more
Open natures door curious cat
And find human harmony
Whether the weather is changing

I WISH I WAS THERE

I wish I was there
When your mother cradled your hair
When your eyes photographed the world
Drifting like baby blue balloons
Up looking at her

I wish I was there
When you fell down the stairs
All seven and suckish
Free falling like rubbish
Down looking at the floor

I wish I was there
When you fancied her, that girl?
When you wanted to try her world
And kiss her slow
Nowhere to go

I wish I was there
I know I hadn't met you yet
I'm the 7th girl you sexed
I'm the 2nd girl you shivered
I'm the 4th to know your house down, 23
I know it's not me that you have only touched
Your memories stretch beyond the brush of imagination

And I wish I was there
To share each one of your years
Your fears of loneliness
Your tears of joy
Your growth pains stuck
That's when you struck me
And I wonder what character I play in your story
In your world, am I another girl?
I wonder what would be, if I knew you at 3?
Would it change a thing?

Would I make your heart sing?
"She's the one"
There is so much of you I have never met
There is so much of you I –
And so, it is true

I wish I was there
I wish it was me

STREET NAMES

To my city of birth, they named their streets
Black Boy Hill and White Ladies Road
I tried to download this information in my mind
But over time it did not make sense
Rated best city, although casted and branded in our dialect
The tongue of former slave owners
Why, it is not that profound
It is just a name to name the ground, they said
But my ancestors lay dead in the thousands
What respect is there?
For symbolism resonates, lingering foul in the air
We would never hear of Jew Lane or Chinese Child Hill
But they accept and abuse our history in the modern day still
It is ever so interesting, for I am within and without
This mockery surmounts, congealing in our mouths
Yet I walk these streets and state these names
Am I also to blame for not protesting a change?
Perhaps it will take a woman this time
Perhaps it will take the eyes of a child
To examine the world wildly
And break the spells with mild aggression
Therefore, let it be a lesson
To keep your eyes open to the reality before your senses
For the earth garden is divided by fences
And our language is burdened by letters
And our skin is judged by possession
To stay awake is our only medicine
To stay blind is to stay trapped in a digital heaven
In my city of birth, they named their streets
Black Boy Hill and White Ladies Road
In the kingdom of spirit each price
Will be delivered and owed

THE WORLD STAGE

Society was swallowed in a shallow end
No capacity to bend the iron bars
Instead to remain stuck cemented
Wishing on stars responsible for decisions
Only to spark from self-centred collisions
Complete weightless skeletons
In a temporary life dance
Musical hypnotic trances to dismiss
The sound, the snake hiss
Never too far away
Never not to play
For the world stage is on fire
And the actors a choir of sorrow
When the spotlight discerns the truth
Pity for the youth who were too fragile to know
Immersed in the world that yearns to show
A new kind of control world order
To entertain the poor fellow behind the border
Artificial, technical designs
Blindfolded their eyes
And unfolded the lies
The thousands upon thousands of lies
Tip toe deep unto the higher realm
By each positive progression
The mind in the third vision is clear
There one can see what one needs
Nutrition for the soul
An external gold bank for the heart
Starting through the aura field
Cleansed transmission of the universe
One strives for a finer tuning
The wave of thought will sing silver
Attracting feathers from the sky
And animals of the night
Listen to the waves flight
That calls for your calling

WORDS

Words are not more than display
A malleable mask of affection
Curving through unnecessary symbol
Like sleep, lays silently spoken
And if not this display
Will ever direct parallel understanding
Only my eyes will ever devise
A pertinent truth
Commanding a vision of self

THE TRIUMPHAL ARCH

It is all for value
Against odd matter
It is all
And there is more,
And there is less.
Forbid we stress
If this present is our gift
And our past is the imprint of our drift
Is not all well?
For bliss or bane
Why drain on against the world?
With our hearts we take human steps,
And we march and we march –
Verging towards without mistake
The triumphal arch

NOISELESS BATTLE

In a state of mind not existing
Memories missed of heeding
Singing without a song
In a noiseless battle cry shaken
Long stretched afar –
Build in the flame of desire;
And caught in breathless needing
A feeling too weak to break
His lusty life force, the cheap taste
Flickered in the needle of sunlight
The clouds behind his back
Mis-matched like the soaks –
Stop. Just sail through
Paddle pushing the tears
Verge the crocodile lane, tempt in tender fears

CARTE BLANCHE

If by yellow nature, so free of will
We, can escape
Heal
Please, give me my right
Know, my wings grow in honour
I take, comfort in my flight
Despite gender or race
The truth, of the new sky will burn lies
Today a colourless mind that leads us
Temptation denies
And, yet we thrive
In an empty bottle we long to fill
I long to, fulfil my possible version
My wishes. A paper blank burden.

YOUNG DESIRE

Crossed between tasteless lust
Or a length love to bind a time of value
To enter slow
Heaven knows I want you
Skin tight, wet bodies, layered there
Do I care enough for more?
To which door do I enter or leave?
To please or to pleasure
I paint pictures in love
I snap paintings in lust
I trust faithlessly in my decision

POLITICAL PUPPETS

Comical political shows
Programmes where puppets play their plans
Up, looking down
The world stage is upside down
Once again, we fall
To base state; Facebook, Instagram
And Snapchat
Information "clouds" pour out
Wiki leaks, data and you
Three o'clock Wednesday
Internet history, you
Search tabs, recents, you
Digital you down to a click
You, a battery player
To serve a game, you
A viewer of the comic tail
They destroyed the Capital
They re-invent a new game
They have a new name
It's been a part of the digital change
Don't fear, listen and learn
Turn to self, remember –
Do you?
Play wise partner
Stay alive

FLY FURTHER AND FAR

Did we know this day would come?
Our youth is dried and undone
But still sour we smile deranged
Gold hearts tainted not unchanged
More curious less refrained
A bright world without old chains
We will fly further and far
Beyond mountains high and stars
Even when our hair is grey
We will remember to play
So, dust off the empty days
Now we know these days have come

NEW LIGHT CALLS

Each tomorrow brings a newborn pleasure
In sweet surrender of being treasured
While sunshine sings to our unsteady hearts
New light calls, clouds descend for us to start
Patterns break as we chase our crystal dreams
We live alive flying above the schemes

LUNA

In the ethereal night her beauty transcended
A moment's patience, her look, a gentle length
Outward across time her thoughts waded
To a spiritual yearning on edge and tense
Cut thread her deepest illusions
She, a raw spread of dark wonder
Through twilight setting sun
In showers and shadows as if in dream
She seems away from her own doing
Opal hopes falling like a stone
She must only remember
Neither hidden or shamed in self
She crossed paths to a lover
To evoke what further away appears near
But alone now her soul lays here
Silent. Through the whisperings
The wandered moon entices
Sweet girl, have no fear

MATERIAL MAYHEM

May I have a glass of stars
A coconut cup of mint deli
On a blue ash tray before the night
As I wear my crew clothing
In velvet coffee design
Right behind the madame in red
Or perhaps instead a simple dish
Inside a white mug a breakfast fish
On ice, still alive and well
Not to eat of course; sparkly suspended
Should I not enjoy my contented friend?
For dessert I admire a banquet of roses
In an orange sky just slight and overdone
My lungs will not contain
All these dusty desires to sustain
For when it is over what did I gain?
None but none

RECYCLED PATTERN

Dancing in wonderland
Juices sweeter than the mind's eye
Let me explore myself, she said
Her song unearthly canned
Pop and out her divinity
Her fizzed reality now blind
She drinks away herself
How delicious and strong the taste
Licked lips wide hips ever expand
She crashes like thrown delph
Her bottle body all used up
She recycles the pattern twice
Reincarnated in a new cover, her expense priced

DOES LOVE CONQUER ALL

I know we will rise and fall on this journey
But if you let me
I'll surrender to all of you
Just tell me what you want
Put my pride aside
If this love is greater
And when my mind denies
I will strive to remember

THE WEIGHT OF DARKER DAYS

My heart bleeds
Wish I could hold natures eternal form
Politics makes me sneeze
Allergic to negative storm –
I can't hide in paradise
When the truth says no
In love with the comfortable
The easy without moan
And I am hungry for life
But tasteless in reach

APRIL

In the spring of April's season
A glow the wonders of beginning
Spiritual horizon in patterns gold
Mystical fragrances ushers in an untold nature
Rebirth, rebuking notions old

Stripped of a tedious life
A divine treasure must unfold
And windows of possibility open to mind
Stretched clear for the heart to find

If it is wanted it will be
Through an undoubted lens
Allow the world to set you free

A SERIES OF COINCIDENCES

Gods that tire of human monotony
Suffering or blurred comedy. And I laugh
Wednesday rain had never been as tropical
Surprising me like a twist of lemon
As I splashed, squeezing past the time
My bus had drove on as soon as I reached the corner
No one but the rain and unseen saw my fate.
Pushing past the moment I tried for another further down but it drove on.
Already full with other souls brewing with morning intention, destination anxiety and tiredness

I was still waiting. My oral exam at nine.
And universal timing did not pity me.
So c'est la vie, I could only think.
I was certain that now I would be spared
But at the crossing a car splashed my blue jeans, two dark stains, emotional pain,
embarrassment. And I was still waiting. 10 past nine I arrived.
I had missed my exam introduction and all the instruction of the day.
I went to the ladies' room to take away my strain and a black spider scattered near me
Oh, dear me, what a day.

END OF EXAMS

I am finally set free towards my destiny
And all troubles have ended
Let loose like a flower from the ground
I bloom and I frown
What should I do now?
So untroubled, I self-create trouble
Escaping any permanent state
Out in the yellow sun
Immediate

NEW WORLDS

Our love never changed
We were placed and directed
I hoped you would remember
That old ways are now
If we could spend time
Collecting the peace of mind
Our puzzle would become clear
It's never too late to ask
We get lost sometimes and plunge
Into portals parallel of oneself
Background space
Just say to me
New motions that drive us
Beat in your heart
And pulse your light
The pictures that you paint
New worlds, no time and –
Sunken impermanence
I'm there

UNTITLED

I think of you as if you are here
As we play different roles and we act with new fears
To think I didn't know you
Memories that have boiled to steam
In the air now is only the love we breathe
Familiar friend we come to play again
In a life that captures and fades
We must love this hovering dream
Flying to ascend the next
As we grow deeper to our highest point
Freer than state
I hope I remember you there

The next selection of 5 poems were written when Allana was in hospital, trying to make sense of her situation.

CURRENTS OF CHANGE

We are divided
Juggling pain and patience
Looking for sunlight
Washing over the falls
But may the tide carry us
Beating through currents of change
Without fear
We take the ride

ILLUSION

We can even grow to love the darkness
That haunts us with illusion
We surrender to both and to all
And when the light fades
The memories in our hearts are brighter
Streaming through the dark tunnel
That encompasses our spirit
Tricks of mind play with our strength
Yet there is no game to our fears
Set aside, gently and remember truly
All you have been given
And the world becomes the greatest gift

FALLING DOMINOES

I have felt fear pushing my heart
Telling me that nothing is safe
And ironically, I create it for myself
For there is nothing to fear
Yet the power of mind strikes
Like falling dominoes
Tipping over each challenge
They fall fast knocking memory after memory
Chasing to the point of nothing
But the pulse of imagination

WE ARE ALL TREASURED

Hidden behind perception
Wide awake all is clear
Like an ocean of stars
The enormity of love
Will expand your own being
The vastness of imagination
Beauty and grace, colours
The day with sunlight
We all infinite sharing
Our gifts of love and sincerity

A STORY TO TELL

We are looked at like rocks
A shell of flesh but
To surprise we have a story to tell
Behind every rock there is gold
A light that sparkles off a navy sea
A beauty unique that serves purpose
That is why every rock is important
For what it becomes is a mystery
A gem a thousand years old
A person to be remembered and told

Printed in Great Britain
by Amazon